CONTENTS

Abacus	3
Banquets	7
Brushes	10
Calligraphy	11
Characters	12
Chess	15
Chinese New Year	19
Chopsticks	21
Clothing	24
Compass	29
Dragon Boat Festival	30
Dragons	33
Dynasties	35
Fans	36
Flag	37
Fireworks	39
Forbidden City	40
Fortune Cookie	43
Fu	45
Games	47
Geography	49
Great Wall	50
Jiao zi	53
Kites	55
Lantern festival	56
Lion Dance	59
Ma Jiang	60
Masks	61
Money	64

Monkey King	65
Moon Cakes	68
Musical Instruments	69
National Anthem	70
Pandas	71
Red envelopes	73
School Life	74
Seal	77
Sports	78
Tea	81
Terracotta Warriors	82
Tian An Men Square	83
Transport	84
Umbrellas	85
Zodiac	86
Zongzi	87

Abacus

People in China began to use an abacus to help them with math problems as early as 500 BC.

The Chinese abacus, known as the *suànpán* 算盤, - "counting tray", is usually 8 inches tall and comes in various widths.

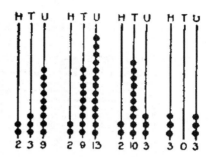

It usually has more than seven rods.
There are two beads on each rod in the upper deck and five beads each in the bottom for both decimal and hexadecimal computation. The beads are usually rounded and made of a hardwood. The beads are counted by moving them up or down towards the beam. If you move them toward the beam, you count their value. If you move away, you don't count their value.

The suanpan can be reset to the starting position instantly by a quick tap along the horizontal axis to spin all the beads away from the horizontal beam at the center.

Learning Activities

1. Make your own Abacus using sticks.

2. Explain to students how to use the Chinese Abacus. Put students into small groups and ask them to present a minute demonstration in Chinese.

3. Ask students to compare a Calculator and an Abacus. Students will list the advantages and disadvantages of both technologies and present findings to the class.

4. Ask students to learn to write the Chinese characters - 算盘. Students will research the radicals included in the characters and create a poster explaining the whole characters.

Language Content

算盘

suànpán

Abacus

Color the Chinese Abacus. Label the numbers in Chinese characters.

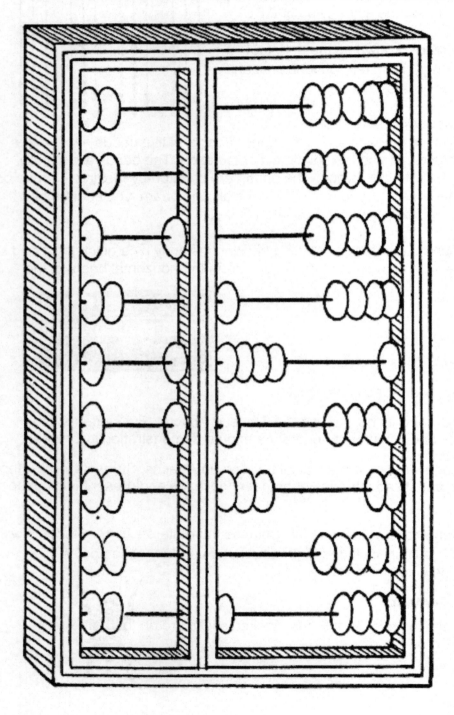

Make your own Abacus

What You Need:
- Pencil
- 9 popsicle sticks
- 56 large pony beads
- 8 4-inch bamboo skewers (if yours are longer, you can cut them to the right length)
- Wood glue

What to Do:
1. Lay three popsicle sticks down so they are parallel. Use the pencil to draw eight matching lines on each stick, evenly spaced and centered across the length of the popsicle sticks.

2. Take the bamboo skewers and align them with the pencil marks. There should be one popsicle stick at each end of the skewers. The third popsicle stick should be in the middle, about 1" away from the one of the end popsicle sticks.

3. Put a thin line of glue on each of the pencil lines you've drawn.

4. Carefully thread seven beads on each of the eight skewers. Place the skewers on the glue lines, arranging the beads so that two beads fall into the 1" space between the two closely placed sticks and the other five fall into the larger space between the middle and end sticks.

5. Let the sticks dry.

6. Glue three popsicle sticks on top of the bamboo skewers so they line up with the sticks below, taking care to keep the beads divided. Let the sticks dry.

7. Glue the last three popsicle sticks on top of the sticks you've just glued down; let dry.

8. Flip the abacus over so that the stacked sticks are on the bottom. Depending on the size of the beads, you may have to add more popsicle sticks to the bottom. The stacked sticks let the beads slide smoothly on the skewers and prevent them from scraping along the surface you're working on.

A - Abacus

The Chinese Abacus was invented to help with Math problems. Can you write the Chinese numbers 1-100?

一								
二								
三								
四								
五								
六								
七								
八								
九								

Banquets

The first course is an even-numbered selection of cold dishes, eight or ten are traditionally served in a Chinese banquet. After the cold course comes a soup such as shark's fin soup or bird's nest soup. The guests help themselves to the dishes at a banquet, but the soup is served by the host, and much drinking and toasting accompanies. Following the soup comes a meat dish. More courses follow -- lobster, pork, scallops, chicken.

Between the courses, a variety of sweets are brought out. Peking duck with scallion brushes, hoisin sauce, and thin pancakes is often served in the middle of the festivities. Traditionally, the final course is a whole fish, which is placed on the table with its head is pointed toward the guest of honor.

Throughout the meal, the guests pay elaborate compliments to the food. Enjoyment of the food offered is much more important than sparkling dinner table conversation. At a banquet, the food itself is the medium communicating the host's good wishes and the joy of the celebration.

Learning Activities

1. Put students into small groups of 6-8. Using clay, ask students to recreate a Chinese banquet. Provide Chinese character labels for the most common food. Students will present their Chinese Banquet to the class, using Chinese.

2. Provide students will a photo of a Chinese banquet. Groups of students will create their own role-play about eating at a Chinese Banquet.

3. Have a Chinese Banquet lunch at your school. Order food from the local Chinese restaurant and label all food in Chinese characters and pinyin. Students will be required to ask for the food using the Chinese names only.

Language Content

北京烤鸭 | 酸辣汤 | 饺子 | 五香鱼 | 面汤 | 烙饼 | 宫保鸡丁 | 皮蛋 | 古老肉 | 米饭 | 火锅

你喜欢吃_____ 吗？

B - Banquets

北京烤鸭 ｜ 酸辣汤 ｜ 饺子 ｜ 五香鱼 ｜ 面汤

烙饼 ｜ 宫保鸡丁｜ 皮蛋 ｜ 古老肉 ｜米饭 ｜

火锅

Draw and label in Chinese your favourite Chinese food:

不好吃！

我喜欢

好吃

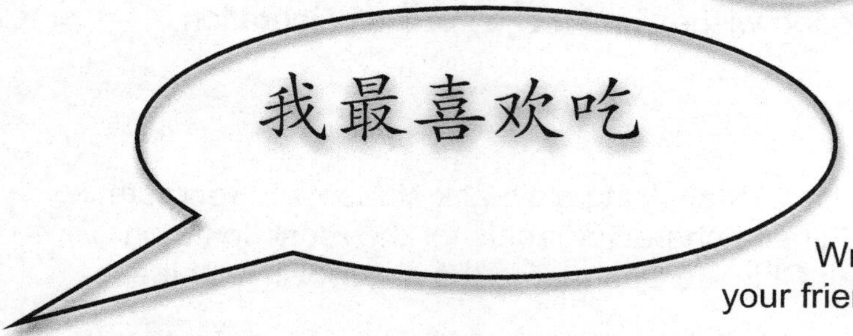

我最喜欢吃

Write sentences in Chinese about your friend's favourite Chinese food:

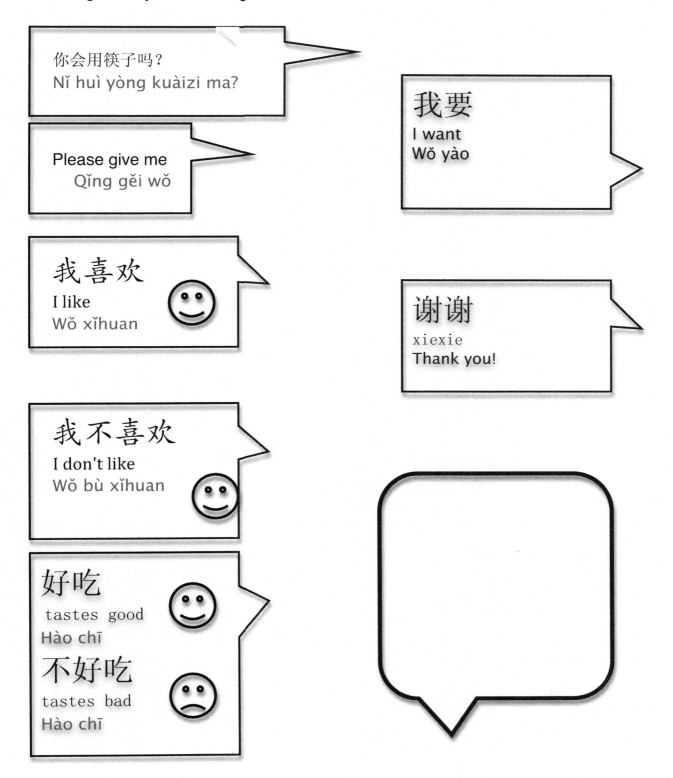

Brushes

Writing Brush

The earliest writing brush that has been found is a relic of the Warring States Period (476 BC – 221 BC). From that time onwards, the brush has evolved into many forms. The nib can be made from rabbit's hair, wool, horsehair, weasel's hair, or bristles, and so on; while the shaft may be made from bamboo, ivory, jade, crystal, gold, silver, porcelain, sandal, ox horn, etc. It is important to see that there can be both soft and hard brushes each producing their own particular styles.

The delicacy gives literators and painters inspiration for creation, and has led to brush shafts being decorated with artistic patterns. One prized example was an ivory-weasel's hair writing brush.
On the ivory shaft with the diameter of 0.8 cm, there carved eight figures of the immortals and pavilions concealed seemingly in the clouds. With this in one's hand, the threads of writing would hardly halt.

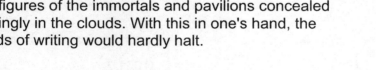

Learning Activities

1. Provide students with a set of Chinese brushes. Demonstrate the use of the brush in calligraphy. Take video of students using the Chinese brushes and post them online to share.

2. Provide students with sheets of red paper. Make scrolls by folding the top and bottom edges of the paper and taping to create a scroll. Allow students to use a Chinese brush to practice writing characters.

3. For younger students, buy a set of cheap writing brushes. Attach a styrofoam head and googly eyes on the top. Students will use this Magic Mo Bi for 'sky-writing' Chinese characters.

Language Content

毛笔
máobǐ

我回写.....
Wǒ huì xiě

Calligraphy

Calligraphy has endured for more than 2,000 years, and evolved into five main ways of writing each with different techniques. Even today, these are still followed and practiced often as a hobby.
Just as calligraphy is an art practiced in western cultures so Chinese writing is a leading component in the four traditional arts, namely lute-playing, chess, calligraphy and painting.

With the unification of the Chinese people by the Qin Dynasty (221 BC – 206 BC) the Prime Minister Li Si actively promoted a unified form of writing based on inscriptions on bronze wares of previous states. This was the first example of calligraphy – known as 'seal character' (Zhuanshu). Calligraphers of seal character stress a slender font, even speed and strength, and even thick lines and strokes. When seen as a whole, this calligraphy is quite round and contracted.

In the Eastern Han Dynasty (25 - 220), people tended to simplify the seal character which had many strokes and created the official script. The new calligraphy appeared to be much neater and delicate, turning the round style into a flat one. When beginning to write a horizontal line, one must let the brush go against the direction of point like a silkworm, and concentrate on stretching steadily, then end up with warp like a swallow's tail.

Learning Activities

1. Give all students a red strip of paper. Demonstrate the writing of a simple Chinese character.

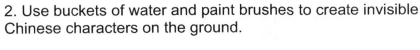

2. Use buckets of water and paint brushes to create invisible Chinese characters on the ground.

3. Make red headbands using red material and calligraphy brushes/ink. Students will practice writing characters on red strips of material and when dry will wear the red headbands!

4. Print Chinese characters. Students will cut them into pieces to make a Character puzzle. Pieces of the puzzle can be stored in envelopes and taken out to put together.

Chinese Characters

Learning Activities

1. Make special Chinese character badges.

2. Make a BIG Chinese Character Book. Students will be given a large sheet of paper with one Chinese character printed on it. Each student will illustrate the character and then all sheets will be stapled together to create a Class Dictionary.

3. Use colored paper to paste over Chinese characters.

4. Allow students to use mini-whiteboards to practice writing characters.

5. Shaving cream words - Spread plastic wrap over a table surface and encourage students to write Chinese characters with their fingers. Wipe over the shaving cream with your hand to begin more characters.

Language Content

你会写汉字吗？ - Can you write Chinese characters?

Make Chinese Characters Badges

What you need:

Pink, White and Red Card Stock
Pattern for Love Card
Pattern for Happiness Card
Pattern for Joy Card
Gold and Red Glitter
Gold and Red Markers
Small Brush
White Glue
Scissors

Instructions

Print characters on card stock. Cut out. Color in the Chinese characters to match the color of the glitter you will be using. Paint the character with white glue and sprinkle on glitter. Let dry. Fold card in half. Write message on inside.

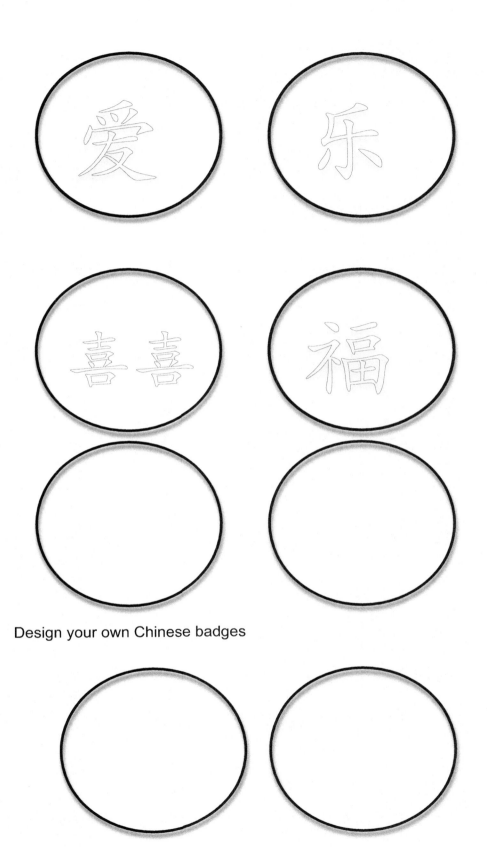

Design your own Chinese badges

14

Characters

Write the Chinese character for each animal of the zodiac.

Chess

Xiangqi is played on a board that is 9 lines wide by 10 lines long. In a manner similar to the game *Wéiqí* 圍棋), the pieces are played on the intersections, which are known as *points*. The vertical lines are known as *files*, while the horizontal lines are known as *ranks*.

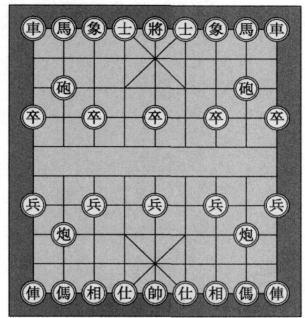

Centered at the first through third ranks of the board is a square zone also mirrored in the opponent's territory. The three point by three point zone is demarcated by two diagonal lines connecting opposite corners and intersecting at the center point. This area is known as 宫 the **palace** or *fortress*.

Dividing the two opposing sides (between the fifth and sixth ranks) is 河 *hé*, the *river*.

Although the river provides a visual division between the two sides, only a few pieces are affected by its presence: "soldier" pieces have an enhanced move after crossing the river, while "elephant" pieces cannot cross.
The starting points of the soldiers and cannons are typically marked with small crosses, but not all boards have these marks.

Learning Activities

1. Using card stock and paper, students will create their own Chinese Chess set.

2. Practice writing the Chinese characters used in the Chinese Chess game.

Language Content

Chinese Chess	象棋	Xiàngqí
Play Chinese Chess	玩中国象棋	Wán zhōngguó xiàngqí

Chess - 象棋

Can you write the Chinese characters used in Chinese Chess?

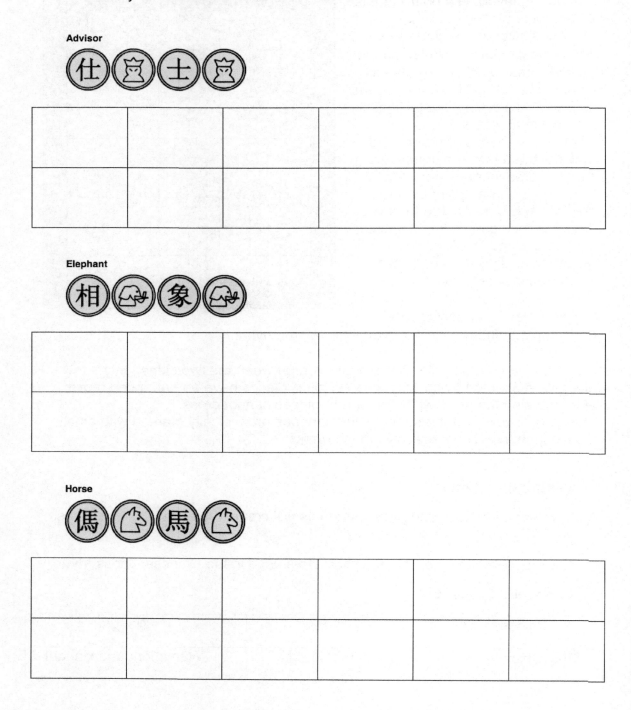

Chariot

俥 車

Cannon

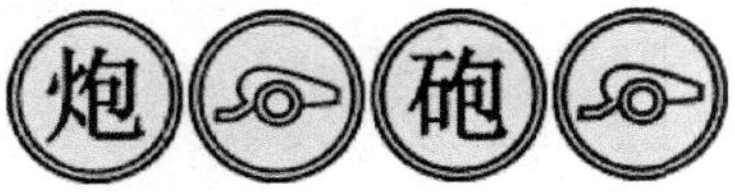

炮 砲

Soldier

兵 卒

Make your own Chinese Chess set.

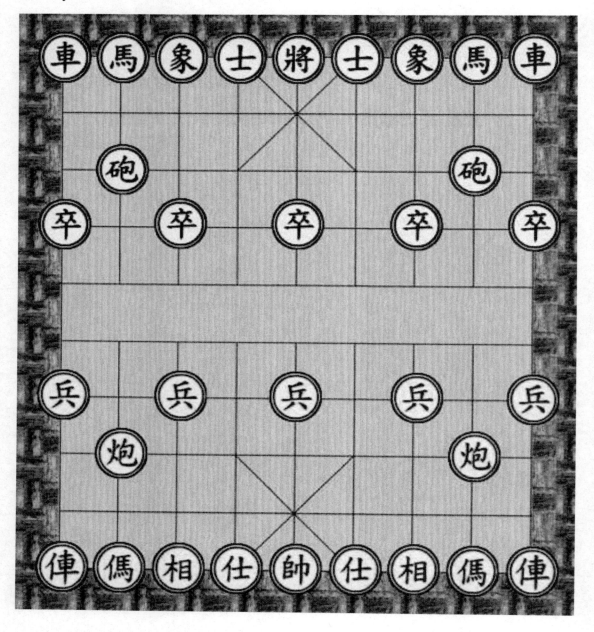

Use bottle tops or coins covered in foil to create your own Chinese Chess pieces.

Chinese New Year

Chinese New Year is a holiday that celebrates the beginning of a new year according to the lunar calendar. It is considered to be one of the most important holidays for Chinese families.

The holiday is celebrated with big family gatherings, gift giving, the eating of symbolic foods and display of festive decorations--all focused on bringing good luck for the new year and celebrating the coming of Spring.

the first day of the New Year it is customary for families to thoroughly clean their homes from top to bottom. Doing this is said to clear out any back luck from the previous year and to ready the house to accept good luck for the coming year.

Another popular custom is to hang up signs and posters on doors and windows with the Chinese word *fu* written on them, which translates to luck and happiness. Buying flowers for the home is also commonplace since they symbolize the coming of spring and a new beginning.

Some popular foods include: dumplings, oranges ("because they are perfectly round, symbolizing completeness and wholeness"), and long noodles ("served to symbolize long life").

Learning Activities

1. Make a red envelope and decorate.

2. Students make a Poster of Chinese New Year symbols.

Language Content

Happy New Year	新年快乐	Xīnnián kuàilè
Congratulations!	恭喜	Gōngxǐ
Good Luck	福	Fú

Sing a Chinese New Year Song

恭喜

每条大街小巷
每个人的嘴里
见面第一句话
就是恭喜恭喜

恭喜恭喜恭喜你呀
恭喜恭喜恭喜你

冬天已到尽头
真是好的消息
温暖的春风
就要吹醒大地

恭喜恭喜恭喜你呀
恭喜恭喜恭喜你

浩浩冰雪融解
眼看梅花吐蕊
漫漫长夜过去
听到一声鸡啼

恭喜恭喜恭喜你呀
恭喜恭喜恭喜你

Chopsticks

The Chinese word for chopsticks is *kuàizi* 筷子.

Chopsticks originated in ancient China as early as the Shang dynasty (1766-1122 BCE).

The earliest evidence of a pair of chopsticks made out of bronze was excavated from near Anyang, Henan, dated roughly 1200 BC.
Held between the thumb and fingers of one hand, chopsticks are used like tongs to pick up portions of food which are prepared and brought to the table in small and convenient pieces. They are thought of as an extension of one's fingers.
Chopsticks are traditionally held in the right hand, even by some left-handed people. Although chopsticks may now be found in either hand, a few still consider left-handed chopstick use improper etiquette. This practice prevents a left-handed chopstick user from accidentally elbowing a right-handed user when seated closely together.

Learning Activities

1. Distribute a bag of M and Ms to each student. Pass out disposable wooden chopsticks. Call out the colors in Chinese, and ask students to use chopsticks to pick up the M and Ms. Use the chopsticks for counting in Chinese as well.

2. Use Page 22 to demonstrate the writing of the two Chinese characters for chopsticks.

3. Use Page 23 to decorate a cover for the chopsticks. Students will write Chinese characters to decorate the cover.

Language Content

你会用筷子吗？

我会用筷子。

Chopsticks

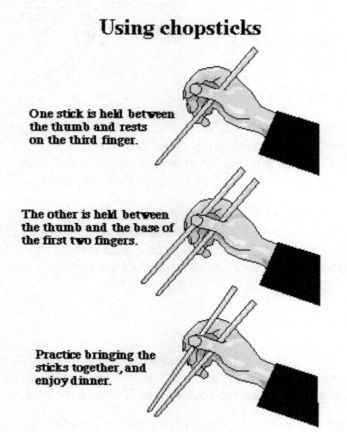

Take the Chopsticks Challenge

1. How many M and Ms can you pick up in 1 minute using chopsticks?

2. In a small group, prepare a short talk in Chinese about how to use chopsticks when eating.

3. Research eating utensils and make a poster showing a time-line of the history of utensils.

4. Decorate a pair of chopsticks with 'tiny' Chinese characters.

5. Create your own Chopsticks Game and play with the whole class.

6. Make your own packet to keep your chopsticks in. Decorate with Chinese characters and designs.

Can you write the Chinese characters for chopsticks?

筷	子	筷	子	筷	子
筷	子	筷	子	筷	子

Chopsticks

Make your own Chopsticks cover

2. Print the file on an A4 size paper.
3. Cut out template. Fold in half by following the dashes in the middle.
4. Color or design your own chopsticks cover using Chinese characters.

Clothing

The ancient Chinese clothing has been influenced by many dynasties. Their mark was distinctly visible in all the dress forms, whether it being the long robes or full sleeves or anything. The ancient clothing mainly conspired of long robes. For women, it was the long tunics touching the ground whereas for men, tunics reaching the knees were mainly worn.

The sleeves were generally very wide and loose. Sashes were added to them as a mark of ornament. Darker shades were generally preferred over the lighter shades. Mostly the common people wore the lighter shades. The yellow color was reserved for the Emperor only. Green, red, white and black were symbols for north, south, east and west.

Learning Activities

1. Make a Poster comparing your own clothes with the clothes worn in Ancient China. Label each piece of clothing.

2. Use the template on Page 25 to dress up a paper doll in traditional Chinese clothing. Describe the clothing to a partner, using Chinese.

3. Pack a suitcase of clothes using the template on Page.....

Language Content

Happy New Year	新年快乐	Xīnnián kuàilè
Congratulations!	恭喜	Gōngxǐ
Good Luck	福	Fú

Color the Chinese clothing. Describe your 2 favorite pictures to your Talk Partner using Chinese.

Clothing

Using paper and colored pencils, create your own Chinese clothing to dress this person. Describe the clothing to a partner, using as much Chinese as you can.

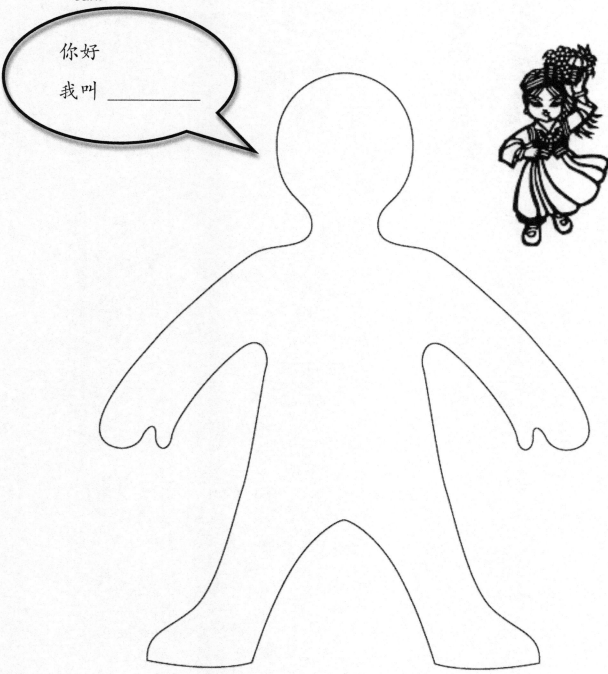

你好

我叫 _____

Clothes

Pack a suitcase of clothes

打包衣服

da bāo yīfú

Tell a friend what clothes you packed.

Remember, only use Chinese!

New Vocabulary

Socks: wà zi 袜子

Shoes: xié zi 鞋子

Pants: kù zi 裤子

Dress: lián yī qun 连衣裙

New Vocabulary

Jacket: jiā kè 夹克

Hat: mào zi 帽子

Who: shéi 谁

Who is wearing? shéi chuān
谁穿

Clothes

Task: Research the school uniforms of your school and a school in China/Taiwan.

Illustrate and include a description of each uniform below. Prepare a short talk about your comparison of school uniforms for the two countries.

Compass

Early in the Spring and Autumn Period (770-476BC), while mining ores and melting copper and iron, Chinese people chanced upon a natural magnetite that attracted iron and pointed fixedly north. In the Warring States Period (206BC-23AD), after constant improvement the round compass came into being. Referred to as a "South-pointer", the spoon- or ladle- shaped compass is of magnetic lodestone, and the plate is of Bronze.

The circular center represents Heaven, and the square plate represents Earth. The handle of the spoon points south. The spoon is a symbolic representation of the Great Bear.

The plate bears Chinese characters which denote the eight main directions of north, north-east, east, etc.

Learning Activities

1. Students can research the first compass invention, and write a description of how the invention differs from a current compass.

2. Using split pins and a circle, create your own compass. Label the four directions in Chinese. Give commands to a partner about which direction they need to walk.

3. Teachers can hide something in the classroom. Students using a paper compass must, follow the directions given by the teacher to find the hidden object. (Use Chinese only)

Compass

Can you write the direction characters for north, east, south and west?

北							
东							
南							
西							

Dragon Boat Festival

端午節
Duānwǔ jié

The festival occurs on the 5th day of the 5th month of the lunar calendar on which the Chinese calendar is based.
The focus of the celebrations includes eating the rice dumpling *zongzi*, and racing dragon boats.

Duanwu commemorates the life and death of the famous Chinese scholar Qu Yuan. He was a loyal minister serving the King of Chu during the Warring States Period in the third century BC. Initially his sovereign favored Qu Yuan, but over time, his wisdom and erudite ways antagonized other court officials. As a result Qu Yuan was accused of trumped-up charges of conspiracy and ejected by his sovereign. During his exile, Qu Yuan composed many poems to express his anger and sorrow towards his sovereign and people.
In the year 278 BC, at the age of 61, Qu Yuan drowned himself. He clasped a heavy stone to his chest and leaped into the water. Knowing that Qu Yuan was a righteous man, the people of Chu rushed to the river to try to save him. The people desperately searched the waters in their boats looking for Qu Yuan but were unsuccessful in their attempt to rescue him. Every year the Dragon Boat Festival is celebrated to commemorate this attempt at rescuing Qu Yuan.
When it was known that Qu Yuan had been lost forever, the local people began the tradition of throwing sacrificial cooked rice into the river for their lost hero. However, a local fisherman had a dream that Qu Yuan did not get any of the cooked rice that was thrown into the river in his honour. Instead the fish in the river were eating the rice. Thus, the locals decided to make *zongzi* to sink into the river in the hopes that it would reach Qu Yuan's body. The following year, the tradition of wrapping the rice in bamboo leaves to make *zongzi* began.

Can you write Dragon Boat?

龙	船		
龙	船		
龙	船		
龙	船		

Design your own Dragon Boat

Dragon Boat festival - Read and answer

Like other Chinese festivals, there is also a legend behind the festival. Qu Yuan served in the court of Emperor Huai during the Warring States (475 - 221 BC). He was a wise and erudite man. His ability and fight against corruption antagonized other court officials. They exerted their evil influence on the Emperor, so the Emperor gradually dismissed Qu Yuan and eventually exiled him. During his exile, Qu Yuan did not give up. He traveled extensively, taught and wrote about his ideas. His works, the Lament (Li Sao), the Nine Chapters (Jiu Zhang), and Wen tian, are masterpieces and invaluable for studying ancient Chinese culture. He saw the gradual decline of his mother country, the Chu State. And when he heard that the Chu State was defeated by the strong Qin State, he was so despaired that he ended his life by flinging himself into the Miluo River.

Legend says after people heard he drowned, they were greatly dismayed. Fishermen raced to the spot in their boats to search for his body. Unable to find his body, people threw zong zi, eggs and other food into the river to feed fish, so hoped to salvage his body. Since then, people started to commemorate Qu Yuan through dragon boat races, eating zong zi and other activities, on the anniversary of his death, the 5th of the fifth month.

Legendary Poet, Qu Yuan

Zong zi is the most popular food for the festival. Zong zi is a special kind of dumpling. It is usually made of glutinous rice wrapped in bamboo leaves. Fresh bamboo leaves are the best for the wrapping since the taste and smell of the fresh bamboo leaves is part of zong zi. Unfortunately fresh bamboo leaves are hard to find.

Today you may see zong zi in different shapes and with a variety of fillings. The most popular shapes are triangular and pyramidal. The fillings include dates, meat, yolk of egg, etc. The most popular fillings are dates. The festival is closely associated with zong zi and dragon boat races. More importantly this is also a national patriot festival through commemorating the great patriot poet, Qu Yuan. People are reminded that the importance of loyalty and commitment to the community in the festival.

Questions

1. What caused Qu Yuan to end his life?
2. How is zong zi made?
3. How would you explain the history of Dragon Boat racing to a friend?
4. What personal qualities are emphasized when remembering QU Yuan?
5. With a partner, design a Poster for the Dragon Boat Festival. Include:
- A brief history of the festivalx
- The Chinese characters for Dragon Boat festival
- Time and date in Chinese
- An illustration of a Dragon Boat

Dragons

Make a Dragon mask.

Did you know?

Chinese dragons ......

Did you know?
- Dragon Years boast the highest childbirth rates in China.
- The more toes a dragon has (up to five) the more "regal" it is.

Did you know?
There are 5 types of Chinese dragons.
Research and find out what they are called:
1.
2.
3.
4.
5.

Design a 'Where's the Dragon Game'. Use Chinese directions to give clues as to where the dragon is hiding.

Can you write the Chinese word for dragon?

龙

Dynasties

Task 1: Create your own Poster of the Chinese Dynasties. Find out the Chinese characters for each name of the Dynasty and label using characters. Include illustrations and information in summary form.

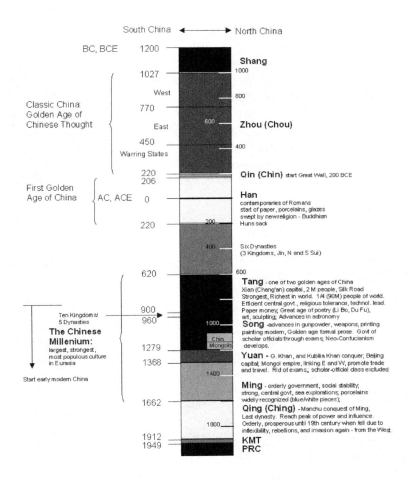

Learning Activity
Task 2: Students will research one Chinese dynasty. They will find out the important events and details of the Dynasty and present the information to the class.
Students will then create a small Booth in the classroom to sell other students their Dynasty. Students may use photos, objects etc., in order to let other classmates know why they think their Dynasty is the best.

Fans

The ancient Chinese loved fans. The earliest fans were made of feathers. One of the ancient Chinese gods,The War God often carried a fan of feathers, although no one knows why. Perhaps he simply liked it.

Over the years, the clever Chinese people made fans from all kinds of materials including straw and wood. But it was not until the Ming Dynasty that the Chinese discovered the art of paper fan folding. They did not invent the folded paper fan. That invention arrived from Japan and Korea on the Ming ships that wandered the earth in search of treasure.

Once the folding paper fan was introduced into ancient Chinese society, it was immediately adopted. Everyone had to have a folded paper fan. Fans were embroidered and painted and decorated and hung. It was more than a fad. It soon became a national activity - nearly everyone made and carried decorated folding paper fans.

Learning Activities

1. Students can make their own Chinese fans and write Chinese characters on them.

2. Set up a Chinese Culture table in your classroom. Display Chinese fans, and encourage students to bring fans from home for the display.

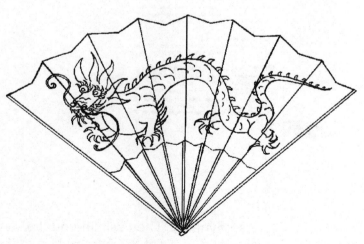

Flag

The **flag of the People's Republic of China** is a red field charged in the canton (upper left corner) with five golden stars. The design features one large star, with four smaller stars in a semicircle set off towards the fly (right side). The red represents revolution; the five stars and their relationship represent the unity of the Chinese people under the leadership of the Communist Party of China (CPC).

The flag was designed by Zeng Liansong, a citizen from Rui'an, Zhejiang.

Learning Activities

1. Give students templates of stars and ask them to create their own Chinese Flag. Attach the flag to a pipecleaner.

2. Introduce the two colors - red and yellow flashcards

3. Ask students to use Chinese to compare the Chinese flag and their own national flag.

Language Content

星 | 红 | 黄 | 国旗

Label your Chinese flag with these Chinese characters: 红 黄

Design your own 中国国旗
What symbols of China will you
use?

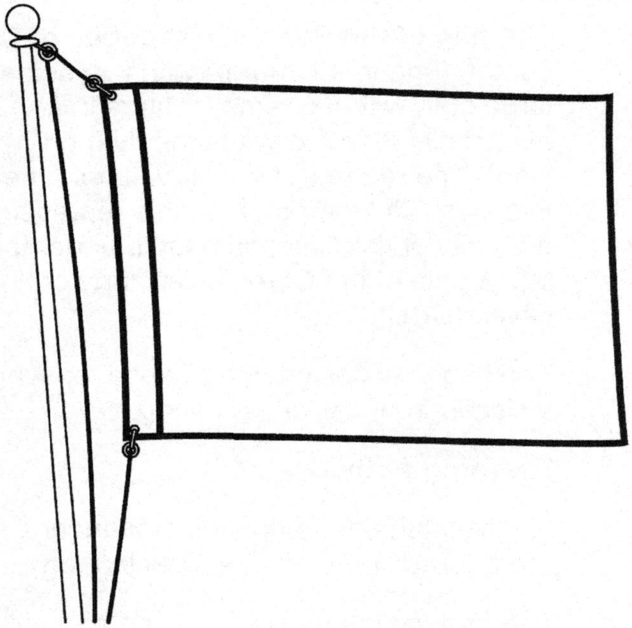

_____

_____

_____

_____

Compare the Chinese flag with your own countries flag.

_____

_____

_____

_____

_____

_____

_____

_____

_____

_____

_____

_____

Fireworks

Rehearse the conversation about Firecrackers with a partner and perform the roleplay to the class.

Firecrackers!

A: 我 要 放 鞭跑!

   wǒ yào fàng biānpào

B: 不行 太 危险 了

   bùxíng tài wéixiǎn le

A: 我 可以 看 你 点 鞭炮 吗?

   wǒ kěyǐ kàn nǐ diǎn biānpào ma?

B: 可以， 不过 你 一定 要 小心 哦!

   kěyǐ, bùguò nǐ yīdìng yào xiǎoxīn o!

A: 知道 了

   zhīdào le

Forbidden City

Construction of the Forbidden City began in relatively modern times, in the year 1406.
The construction took an estimated one million workers 14 years to build hundreds of perfect and beautiful buildings. The Forbidden City served as the seat of government for the Ming Dynasty.
Today, it is a museum.

There are 800 buildings that have in total about 9,999 rooms. The Forbidden City is the world's largest palace complex. Millions of people visit this incredible place each year and gaze in awe.

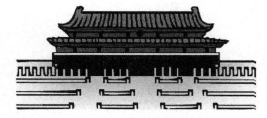

Learning Activities

1. Students will make their own paper Forbidden City using the URL below in the Resources section.

2. Students will choose one section of the Forbidden City to research and present a role-play helping a tourist who is lost in the Forbidden City find their way out.

3. Students can research the Forbidden City online and gather photos. They will use photos and text to create a virtual tour presentation about the City.

Language Content

故宫
Gùgōng

Resources
Make your own paper Forbidden City
http://cp.cij.com/en/contents/3152/03345/index.html

Virtual Forbidden City
http://www.beyondspaceandtime.org/

Forbidden City - 故宫

A Meridiian Gate
B Gate of Supreme Harmony
C Hall of Supreme Harmony
D Hall of Central Harmony
E Hall of Preserving Harmony
F Hall of Heavenly Peace
G Hall of Terrestrial Peace
H Imperial Garden
I XiHua Gate
J DongHua Gate
K Watch Tower

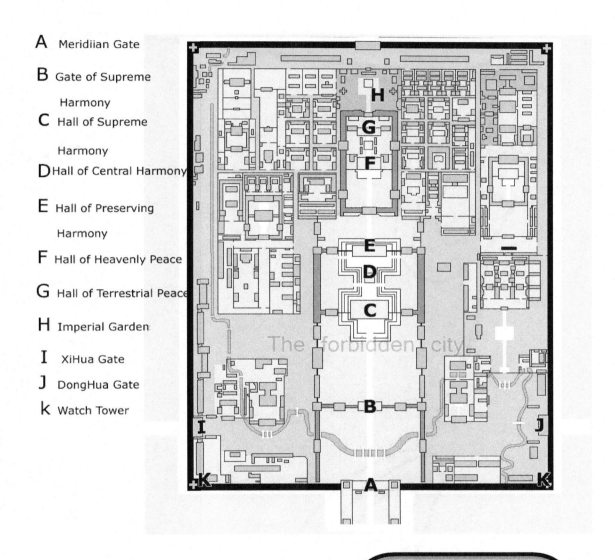

Hall of Supreme Harmony (太和殿),

Hall of Central Harmony (中和殿)

Hall of Preserving Harmony (保和殿).

Can you answer this question in Chinese?

故宫到底有多少间房？

My Visit to the Forbidden City

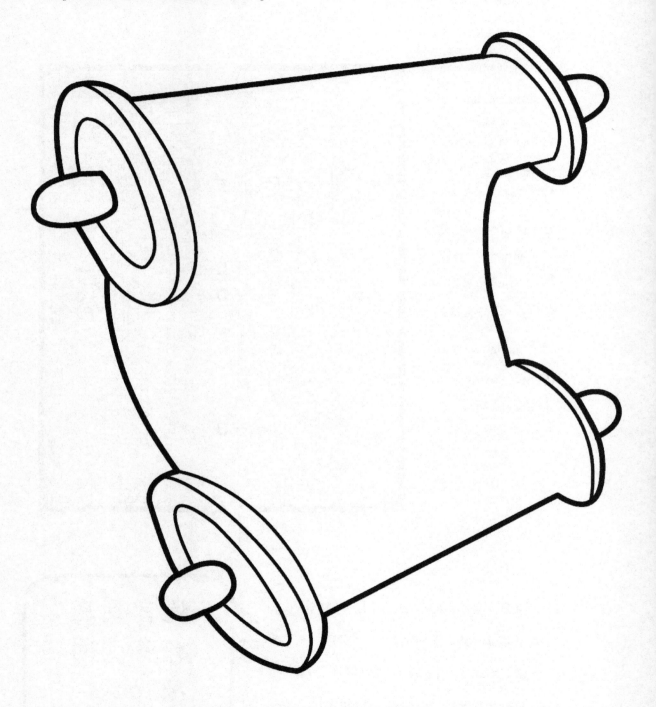

Write a Diary entry on the scroll. Describe the Forbidden City in your own words.

Fortune Cookies

Ingredients

2 large egg whites
1/2 teaspoon pure vanilla extract
1/2 teaspoon pure almond extract
3 tablespoons vegetable oil
8 tablespoons all-purpose flour
1 1/2 teaspoons cornstarch
1/4 teaspoon salt
8 tablespoons granulated sugar
3 teaspoons water

How to Make the Easy Chinese Fortune Cookie Recipe

STEP ONE:
~ heat oven to 425 degrees
~ grease a baking sheet.
~ put egg white into a bowl and lightly beat
~ add vanilla extract, almond extract and vegetable oil until frothy
~ do not beat until stiff, just frothy
~ in another bowl add sifted flour, salt sugar and cornstarch,
~ to in this flour mixture add water and blend well
~ into the egg white mixture and the flour mixture and stir until a smooth fortune cookie dough mixture emerges
~ the fortune cookie batter should drop easily of a spoon but not be runny
~ scoop a small piece of batter onto the cookie baking sheet
~ try and leave at least 3" space around them as they will grow larger
~ Move the baking sheet with a rocking motion to and fro so the batter forms little circles (approx 2" in diametre)

~ bake the little fortune cookies until the outer 1/2-inch of each cookie turns golden brown and they are easy to remove from the baking sheet with a spatula (14 - 15 minutes).

 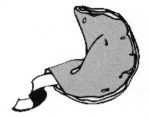 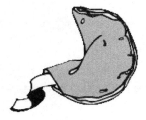

**Fortune Cookies -
Make messages**

新年快乐

你叫什么名字？

祝你生日快乐

Fu

Fu is a lucky word. It is very easy to say it.
Around the Chinese New Year, people often put up a poster with this word on it - upside down! It's the only time when a Chinese word is posted upside down intentionally. Like this:
Since the Ming Dynasty (600 years ago), a large *fu* character would oftenbe found at the entrances of houses to bring a continuous flow of good luck through the door.
Usually written in black ink on red diamond-shaped paper, *fu* is affixed upside down.
This is because the phrase **"to turn upside down"** *dao4*, is also a pun on the word **"arrived"** *dao4*.
An upside down *fu* therefore means **"Luck has arrived"**.
This good luck symbol is a popular decoration during Chinese New Year.

Learning Activities

1. Students create their own 'Fu' Poster for their home.

2. Students use the 'Fu' character to make their own jigsaw puzzle.

3. Make a stand up paper cut of the word - Fu using colored paper.

Make a jigsaw from the poster. Color and cut out into 10 pieces.

Give it to a friend to rearrange!

Design your own T Shirts with the Chinese character for good luck!

Games

Jiànzi (毽子), **ti jian zi** (踢毽子), **ti jian** (踢毽) or **jiànqiú** (毽球) is a traditional Asian game in which players aim to keep a heavily weighted shuttlecock in the air using their feet and other parts of the body (but not hands,

Jian zi — Make your own!

Making and Playing *Jianzi* (Chinese shuttlecock)

Materials needed:
- A quarter or washer
- Straw
- Scissors
- Real feather or paper feather (see template)
- Duct tape

Procedure

1. Place the quarter on duct tape.

2. Cut the straw about one inch, and cut several slits (1/4 inch in length) at the bottom.

3. Open the end of the straw with the cuts, and plant it onto the quarter.

4. Cut the duct tape in the center and secure the straw on both sides.

5. Insert the feathers, and play!

Games - Rock, Paper, Scissors

In the late Ming period, warlords of Later Han played a game called shoushiling, which is considered to be Rock, Paper, Scissors. Shoushiling can be translated as "hand-command."

- **Rock**, represented by a clenched fist.
- **Scissors**, represented by two fingers extended and separated.
- **Paper/cloth**, represented by an open hand, with the fingers connected (horizontal).

- Rock blunts or breaks scissors: that is, rock defeats scissors
- Scissors cut paper: scissors defeats paper
- Paper covers cloth or captures rock: paper defeats rock

rock 石头 shí tou

scissors 剪刀 jiǎn dāo

cloth 布 bù

	我 输了 Wǒ shū le	我 赢了 Wǒ yíng le

Write on the chart above, the times you won and lost during the game!

Geography of China

Capital: Beijing

Population: 1,313,973,713

Total Size: 9,596,960 square km

Size Comparison: slightly smaller than the US

Geographical Coordinates: 35 00 N, 105 00 E

World Region: Asia

General Terrain: mostly mountains, high plateaus, deserts in west; plains, deltas, and hills in east

Geographical Low Point: Turpan Pendi -154 m

Geographical High Point: Mount Everest 8,850 m

Climate: extremely diverse; tropical in south to subarctic in north

Learning Activities

1. Create a floor size Map of China. Give students labels of cities and famous places. Ask students to place the labels on the Map. Brainstorm how students can travel from city to city. Draw and label ways to travel to add to the map. Weather conditions can also be added to the floor map for future reference.

2. Use direction vocabulary to find places on a Chinese map. The teacher will use the words - 旁边，在前面 etc., and students will mark the places on the large map of China.

3. The teacher will write all the Provinces of China on slips of paper. Groups of students will receive one strip of paper and research the area. They will present a persuasive talk to the class, as to why their province is the BEST in China.

Great Wall

The Chinese worked on the Great Wall for over 1700 years. In turn, each emperor who came to power added pieces of the wall to protect their dynasties. But the wall was not a solid wall. It was a line of disconnected barricades.
First Emperor Qin wanted a much better barricade to protect his people from the Mongol invaders to the north. He wanted a strong wall 30 feet wide and 50 feet high.

First Emperor Qin used peasants, captured enemies, criminals, scholars, and anyone else who irritated him, and put them all to work building the Great Wall. Laborers were not paid for their work. It was slave labor.
About 3000 people worked on the wall during the Qin Dynasty. Rocks fell on people. Walls caved in. Workers died of exhaustion and disease. Laborers were fed only enough food to keep them alive. There is an old Chinese saying, "Each stone in the wall represents a life lost in the wall's construction.
This project continued long after First Emperor Qin's death. Building the wall was a project that continued for many hundreds of years until the wall was over 3700 miles long. Most emperors used the same system that Qin used, forced labor.

Learning Activities

1. Students create their own Great Wall using clay or playdough. Labels can also be included to show important information. Students will present their Great Wall to the whole class in a short presentation.

2. Students will work in small groups to research information about the Great Wall. They will produce a brochure for tourists explaining the history of the Wall.

3. Students will use the Great Wall ticket to design their own ticket using Chinese characters.

4. Students will rehearse language needed when lost! They will role-play the 'Maps for Sale' conversation.

Language Content

长城

Chángchéng

Great Wall of China

Can you write the Characters for Great Wall?

长	城	长	城	长	城
长	城	长	城	长	城

Information I found out about the Great Wall:

A Ticket to the Great Wall

Research what a ticket to the Great Wall looks like.

Design your own below using Chinese characters:

If you became lost on the Great Wall, how would you ask for directions?

Jiao zi

Jiaozi typically consist of a ground meat and/or vegetable filling wrapped into a thinly rolled piece of dough, which is then sealed by pressing the edges together or by crimping. Jiaozi should not be confused with wonton: jiaozi have a thicker, chewier skin and a flatter, more oblate, double-saucer like shape and are usually eaten with a soy-vinegar dipping sauce (and/or hot chili sauce); while wontons have thinner skin, are sphere-shaped, and are usually served in broth. The dough for the jiaozi and wonton wrapper also consist of different ingredients.

Learning Activities

1. Students a simple conversation skit to talk about making jiao zi.

2. Watch a video of the making of jiǎozi online. Ask students to research words needed to explain how to make jiǎozi. In small groups, students will record the simple explanation and present the recording to the class.

Language Content

饺子 jiǎozi

Can you write the Chinese word for dumplings?

饺子	饺子	饺子	饺子	饺子
饺子	饺子	饺子	饺子	饺子
饺子	饺子	饺子	饺子	饺子
饺子	饺子	饺子	饺子	饺子

Jiao zi Recipe

Ingredients for 35-40 dumplings
Wrappers
- 500 g (18 oz.) flour
- 270 g (10 oz.) water

Filling
- 300 g (10 oz.) ground pork
- 150 g (5 oz.) Chinese cabbage, minced
- 2 bunches of cilantro, chopped
- 100 g (3 1/2 oz.) ginger, chopped
- 2 cloves of garlic, chopped
- 1 tbsp. dark soy sauce
- 1 tbsp. sesame oil

Method

1. Combine the flour and water; roll the dough out thinly on a work surface.

2. Using a cutter, cut out rounds 12 cm (5") in diameter.

3. Combine the ingredients for the filling.

4. Place a small amount of filling in the center of each dough circle and fold over to form a plump semi-circle.

5. Usually the traditional crescent moon shape is chosen. In this case, using the thumb and index finger of your right hand, roll the border of each dumpling, then using the thumb and index finger of each hand, press lightly to form the crescent. This step is called "modeling happiness." In some families, both ends are joined by curving the shape more in order to give it the shape of a silver ingot.

6. Place the dumplings one at a time into a large pot of boiling water; once they rise to the surface, drain and transfer to a plate.

7. Combine the ingredients for the sauce; serve in small individual dishes.

Kites

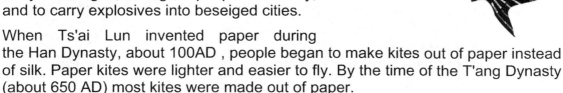

The earliest kites were probably invented in China about 800 BC, during the Chou Dynasty. People made these early kites out of bamboo and silk. Chinese people flew kites for fun, and also used kites in war to carry messages, to signal people far away, and to carry explosives into beseiged cities.

When Ts'ai Lun invented paper during the Han Dynasty, about 100AD , people began to make kites out of paper instead of silk. Paper kites were lighter and easier to fly. By the time of the T'ang Dynasty (about 650 AD) most kites were made out of paper.

The four most common types of Chinese kites are:

-Centipede (multiple flat sections stacked together plus a 'head')
-Rigid Winged (paper or silk tightly stretched over rigid spars)
-Soft Winged (flexible structures behind just one spar)
-Flat (just like the name says)

Make your own kite

What you need:
1 two foot long stick or rod
1 three foot stick or rod
1 large sheet of newspaper or extra craft paper
String (lots of tied shoelaces works!)
Scissors
Glue

What you do:
Place your two sticks/rods together so that they cross. With string, tie the two together where they join. Wrap it around several times so it is secure. Cut a notch into the four ends of the sticks. Wrap a piece of string around the cross making sure to string around each of the four notches. This will be your kite's frame when you're done. Place your paper on a flat surface and cut around the shape of the kite. Leave two or three inches of extra space when you cut. Fold the excess paper over the frame and glue it down. Tie a long piece of string to the inner frame and make it as long as you wish.

Lantern Festival

This holiday is celebrated approximately 15 days after the start of the Chinese New Year.

There are many wonderful stories about how the Lantern Festival first began. One story is that in ancient times, people would go in search of spirits with burning sticks. They thought the spirits could be seen during a full moon. Another is about a lonely young girl, in Han times, who tricked an emperor into having a wonderful festival just so she could visit with her family! The emperor had such a good time, he decided to make this festival an annual event!

By T'ang times, many families simply set aside one evening, during the first full moon after the new year, to honor the moon. They would sit outside, and gaze up, in awe and delight.

Today, people wear white in honor of the moon, lanterns are hung in the malls and markets, and children carry paper lanterns to school, to light their way to a bright and happy future.

Learning Activities

1. Students create their own lantern and decorate with Chinese characters.

Lantern Making

Chinese Lantern From Paper
灯笼
Dēnglóng

Make a Paper Lantern

Chinese lantern paper craft. Fold a rectangular piece of paper in half. Make a long and thin rectangle, and cut it. Don't cut all the way to the edge of the paper. Then unfold the paper. Glue the edges of the paper together.
Make and glue the handle of the lantern.

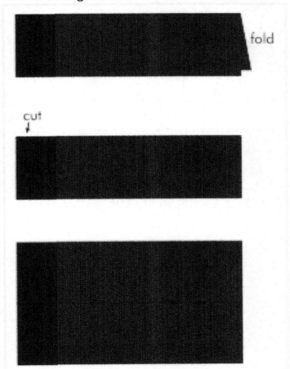

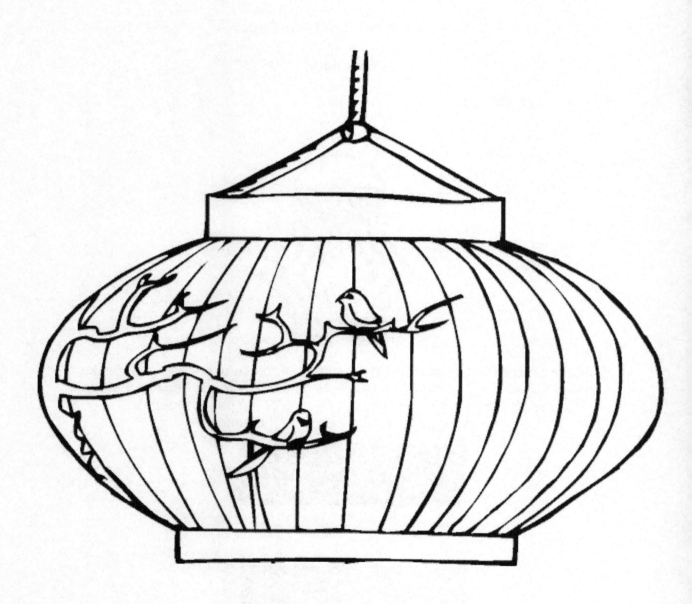

Use Chinese characters to decorate the lantern.

Lion Dance

The Lion Dance is a form of traditional dance in Chinese culture, in which performers mimic a lion's movements in a lion costume. The lion dance is often mistaken as dragon dance. An easy way to tell the difference is that a lion is operated by two people, while a dragon needs many people.

Also, in a lion dance, the performers' faces are covered, since they are inside the lion. In a dragon dance, the performers can be seen since the dragon is held upon poles

Learning Activities

舞狮

wǔ　shī

Ma Jiang

Learning Activities

1. Students create their own MaJiang pieces to play with.

2. Students watch a video online about how to play Majiang.

Design your Ma jiang pieces below:

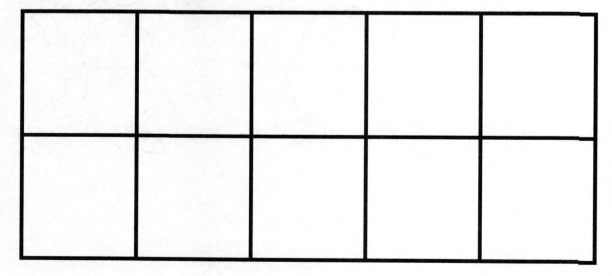

Masks

The origins of Chinese masks are rooted in ancient religious shamanism. Over the centuries and many generations, artists refined the use of colors on Chinese masks. Today, color continues to be used to indicate emotions or give clues about the identity of a character.

Types of Chinese Masks

There are several types of Chinese masks: dancer's masks, masks for festive occasions, masks for newborns, masks designed to keep homes safe and theatrical masks. When used on the stage, masks help viewers determine, at a glance, the attributes of a theatrical character. Masks are usually made from wood. However, Chinese opera masks, possibly the style that is best known in the west, are actually painted on actors' faces.

Chinese Masks and Color Meanings

Many colors are used in any given Chinese mask, but the dominant colors impart specific characteristics.

- Red used on masks indicates a positive character. Red can also mean prosperity, loyalty, courage and heroism. Red shows intelligence and bravery.
- Purple is sometimes used as a substitute for red. In its own right, purple can represent justice and sophistication.
- Black means that the character is neutral. Black also indicates impartiality and integrity.
- Blue faces are also an indication of neutrality. In addition, blue can show stubbornness, astuteness and fierceness.
- Green shows that the character is violent, impulsive and lacks restraint.
- Yellow tells the audience that the character is cruel. Yellow can also mean evil, hypocritical, ambitious or sly.
- White faces indicate that the character is evil and hypocritical.
- Gold and silver show the audience that the character is a god or a demon. The character also may be a ghost or a spirit. Gold and silver symbolize mystery.

Learning Activities

1. Students will create their own Chinese Opera masks.

2. Students will research Chinese Opera and design a poster in Chinese. (include time of performance, location, cost etc.,)

Masks

Color the Chinese Opera Masks

With a Talk partner, explain what colors need to be used to color the masks above. Only use Chinese colors to describe each mask.

红色　绿色　蓝色　白色　黄色　黑色

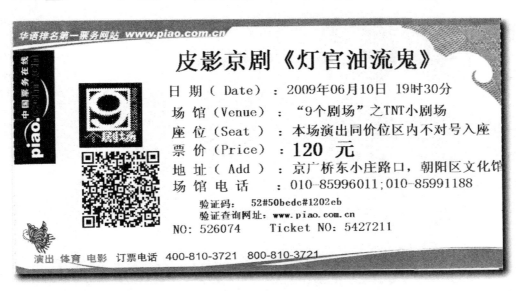

Money

The **Renminbi** 人民币 is the official **currency** of the **People's Republic of China**.
It is abbreviated as RMB, and the units for the Renminbi are the yuan (元), jiǎo (角), and fēn (分)
Cowry shells are believed to be the earliest form of currency used in Central China, about 3000 to 4500 years ago.
The Chinese seemed to invent the first metal coins before 900 BC.

As part of the Unification of China, Qin Shi Huang 秦始皇; *Qín Shǐ Huáng*, 260 BC – 210 BC) abolished all other forms of local currency and introduced a national uniform copper coin based on the coins previously used by Qin. These coins were round with a square hole in the middle which remained the common design for most Chinese copper coins until the 20th century.

Learning Activities

To make these Chinese coins (much bigger than real ones), shape them out of clay and then paint on the Chinese characters. Chinese coins usually had square holes in the middle so you could keep them on a ribbon or a stick. Design your own Chinese coins using the blank templates

Monkey King

Sun Wukong, also known as the **Monkey King**, is a main character in the classical Chinese epic novel *Journey to the West* (西遊記). In the novel, he is a monkey born from a stone who acquires supernatural powers through Taoist practices. After rebelling against heaven and being imprisoned under a mountain by the Buddha, he later accompanies a monk on a journey to India.

Learning Activities

1. Students can examine the Monkey King stamps below, and create their own Monkey King stamps.

2. Students will make a list of all the actions Monkey King can do.

Language Content

孙 悟 空
Sūn Wùkōng

西游记 Xīyóujì Journey to the West

这是谁？

这是 孙悟空 - Sūn Wùkōng

他会做什么？

爬山

说话

唱歌

玩

笑

跑

用筷子

哭

How well do you know Monkey King and Pigsy?

Draw each the following two characters from the story and use the Chinese words below to describe each one.

孙悟空

Draw 孙悟空 - Sūn Wùkōng

Draw Pigsy 猪八戒 Zhu Bajie

快乐　　非常　　胖

矮　真　奇怪　比较

一边....一边

Moon Cakes

月餅

Simple Moon Cake Recipe for kids
Ingredients:
- 1/4 cup sugar
- 2 egg yolks
- 1/2 cup salted butter
- 1 cup all-purpose flour
- 1 cup strawberry (or your favorite) jam (traditionally red bean paste is used so if you want a more authentic version, you can use a can of red bean paste instead of the jam)

Directions:
1. Preheat the oven to 375 degrees.
2. Combine the butter, sugar and 1 egg yolk and stir.
3. Mix in the flour.
4. Form the dough into one large ball and wrap it in plastic wrap
5. Refrigerate dough for half an hour.
6. Unwrap the chilled dough and form small balls in the palms of your hand.
7. Make a hole with your thumb in the center of each moon-cake and fill with about half a teaspoon of jam.
8. Brush each cake with the other beaten egg yolk and place on a cookie sheet. (We didn't have a brush to do this, so skipped the brushing step)
9. Bake for about 20 minutes or just until the outside edges are slightly brown.

Taste Test - Moon Cakes

名字	喜欢	不喜欢	好吃	不好吃

Musical Instruments

Students create their own Chinese Musical Instruments poster.

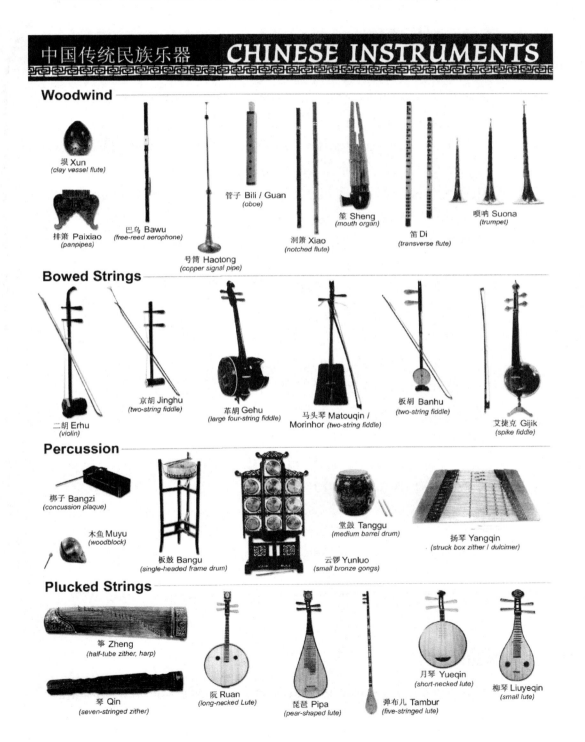

National Anthem

起来！不愿做奴隶的人们！

Stand up! those who are unwilling to become slaves!

把我们的血肉，筑成我们新的长城！

Take our flesh, and build it to become a new Great Wall!

中华民族到了最危险的时候，

The Chinese people have reached a most dangerous time,

每个人被迫着发出最后的吼声。

Every person is being compelled to send issue a final roar.

起来！起来！起来！

Arise! Arise! Arise!

我们万众一心，

We are millions with one heart,

冒着敌人的炮火，前进

Braving our enemy's gunfire, march on!

冒着敌人的炮火，前进！

Braving our enemy's gunfire, march on!

前进！前进！进!

March on! March on! Charge!

Learning Activity

1. Create a video with 5 classmates singing the Chinese National Anthem.

Pandas

Giant pandas have lived in the bamboo forests of China for millions years and have been honored by the Chinese for a very long time. In fact, giant pandas have appeared in Chinese art for thousands of years. Because the giant panda is considered a national treasure in China, it is protected by law so that it does not become extinct.

The Giant Panda is white and black. An adult can grow to 3 1/2 to five feet and weigh up to 350 pounds. In the wild, adult female pandas give birth once a year and usually produce two cubs in the litter? A newborn cub will weigh around 5 ounces is all white and blind at birth. The black spots develop after about a month. A cub will begin to eat bamboo at about six months and be fully weaned after nine months. At the end of the first year they are about 70 to 80 pounds. The cubs will stay with their mother for about 1 1/2 years. A Panda reaches maturity at five to seven years and live in the wild for about 25 years.

Giant Pandas live on mountainous slopes in western China and Eastern Tibet. Sichuan province is home to many of these bears. Because of their limited number, there are very few in zoos. The main diet is bamboo shoots. They will also eat a small amount of fish and rodents. They range in very small areas, of about one square mile. Females range in even smaller areas.

Learning Activities

1. Make a Panda Mask using the template.
2. Make badges for your friends with the words - 我爱熊猫 on them.

Language Content

熊猫
Xióngmāo

Make a Panda mask.

Introduce your Panda in Chinese.

Use the following language: 你好，我叫................ 我.......岁。

Red envelopes

Red envelopes are mainly presented at social and family gatherings such as weddings or on holidays such as the Chinese New Year.

The red of the envelope symbolizes good luck and is supposed to ward off evil spirits.

The act of requesting for red packets is normally called

討紅包, 要利是,

Learning Activities

1. Students create their own Red Envelopes.

Make your own Red Envelope. Color and decorate with Chinese characters.

School Life

In China, there are six years of elementary school, three years of middle school, and three years of high school. There is an exam at the end of middle school to decide who attends high school. Only 30 percent of middle school students go on to high school.

School begins around 7:30 with a flag raising ceremony and a lecture from the principal who speaks through a bullhorn. Describing the first day of school in a small town school, Peter Hessler wrote in The New Yorker, "The loudspeakers crackle, and music came on for the flag-raising. The older children, wearing the red kerchiefs of the Young Pioneers, marched in place while the national anthem played."

Morning exercises at an elementary school
Children typically go to school from 7:00am to 4:00pm. Elementary school begins at 7:30am. They study mathematics, reading, writing and propaganda, and often write on thin, brittle paper that feels like onion skin and glows if held up to the light. During recess children do calisthenics and relaxation exercises that consist of pressing two finger on one's eyes, nose or cheeks.

A typical school has few academic and athletic facilities other than a chalkboard, some desks, chairs and a Chinese flag and courtyard where children play. Better schools have a dirt soccer field. Few schools have air conditioning or heating. In the winter, teachers and students are often bundled up in heavy coats and gloves in the classrooms, their breath forming clouds.

Middle class children fill the hours after school with homework, music lesson and other enrichment programs. English classes and math Olympics are popular. Parents spend sizable chunks of money on classes at computer schools and language academies. Children often have lots of homework, which they often do in copybooks in front of their parents.

Learning Activites

1. Students compare school life in China and in their own country. Make a podcast about your daily routine at school and compare with a Chinese school.

2. Choose any 5 Tasks to complete below.

All about my School - Learning Tasks

1. Write a Rap using: 喂，什么事？Include at least 5 classes you study at school in the Rap. Record the Rap and burn onto a CD.

2. Conduct a "Things I study at school" Interview with a classmate in Chinese. Write the Questions you want to ask (in Chinese) and record the answers on a "Class Schedule" Table.

3. Create a BINGO Game using at least 10 School Subjects. Play The BINGO Game with 4 classmates in Chinese.

4. Use a Map of your school (drawn or real image) and label the different rooms and areas. Conduct a virtual tour through the school and record the Virtual Tour using Audacity.

5. Conduct a Survey of your classmates' favorite School Subject. Use Chinese to ask the questions and record your findings in Chinese characters on a Graph Poster.

6. Create a set of 5 Bumper Stickers that use 5 different Subjects and a sentence about each one.

7. Design a Poster advertising your School in Chinese characters. Include 8 Subject areas and why students should study at your school.

8. Create a Mini-Comic story – "A Day in the Life of…" The Comic will include times, activities of a typical school day for a 13 year-old student at your school.

9. Develop and make a Matching Card Game using all Schools subjects Vocabulary words in this Unit of Work. (Characters and Pinyin and English)

kè
class/classes: 课

shu xué kè
Math class: 数 学 课

dì lǐ kè
Geography class: 地 理 课

tǐ yu
P.E: 体 育

hua xué
Chemistry: 化 学

School Life - In Chinese schools, students study the same subjects as other children in the US, UK, and Australia. However, Chinese students do not have any choices in the subjects they must study. Examinations are very important in the Chinese educational system. Students go to extra classes and study long hours so they can do well in the final exams.

	一	二	三	四	五
第一節					
第二節					
第三節					
第四節					
第五節					
第六節					
第七節					

Chinese students usually begin the day with morning exercises, which are done to music. During the day, a time is also set aside for eye exercises.

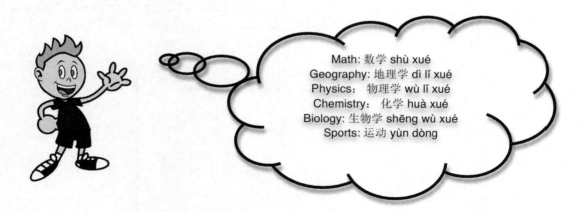

Math: 数学 shù xué
Geography: 地理学 dì lǐ xué
Physics: 物理学 wù lǐ xué
Chemistry: 化学 huà xué
Biology: 生物学 shēng wù xué
Sports: 运动 yùn dòng

Seal

A **seal**, is a general name for printing stamps and impressions that are used instead of signatures in personal documents.

Chinese seals are typically made of stone, sometimes of metals, wood, bamboo, plastic, or ivory, and are typically used with red ink or cinnabar paste.

The role of seals in the Chinese culture can hardly be overestimated. For the last 3,000 years they have been used in official, private, even magic spheres. The earliest examples of seals come from the Shang dynasty (BCE 16-11 c.) from the archeological sites at Anyang. Very little is known, however, about their usage at this early stage, it is only starting from the Spring and Autumn period (BCE 722-481) that we begin to see an increased quantity of seals paired with textual references to them. According to a Han dynasty story, the first seal was given to the Yellow Emperor by a yellow dragon with a chart on its back. Another story says that it was given to Emperor Yao by a phoenix as the emperor was sitting in a boat. In any case, the receipt of the seal signifies the conferral of the Mandate of Heaven. He who has the seal possesses the Mandate of Heaven, in other words, he has been given the right to rule the empire. So when Tang, the first ruler of the Shang dynasty overthrows the last tyrant of the previous Xia dynasty, he seizes the royal seal and thus establishes his power.

Learning Activity

1. Using a carrot or a potato, carefully carve out the shape of a Chinese character. Stamp the carved potato with paint to make your own seal.

Sports in China

Football, basketball, and table tennis are the main sports in China.
The People's Republic of China has emphasized sports and the government funds and trains young talented players into professional players.

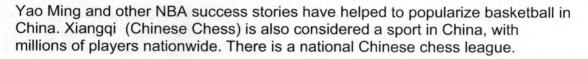

Ping pong is one of the biggest amateur recreational sports in China today, with an estimated 200 million players.
Badminton is also well established and quite popular in China.

Yao Ming and other NBA success stories have helped to popularize basketball in China. Xiangqi (Chinese Chess) is also considered a sport in China, with millions of players nationwide. There is a national Chinese chess league.

Taijiquan is a kind of Chinese boxing, combining control of breath, mind and body. It emphasizes body movement following mind movements, tempering toughness with gentleness and graceful carriage. Qigong is a unique Chinese way of keeping fit. It aims at enhancing health, prolonging life, curing illness and improving physiological functions by concentrating the mind and regulating the breath.

Learning Activities

1. Students will research popular sports in China and design a flyer to distribute among their classmates.

2. Students will write an Interview script to interview a famous sports player.

3. Students will conduct a survey about what sports their classmates like using 你喜欢什么运动？

4. Students will research sports playing during the Olympic Games and create a podcast of when and where 10 of their favorite sports are being played. (in Chinese)

Sports in China

Rehearse the sports vocabulary and create your own Rap about your favorite sports.

Interview a Sports Person

You will Interview a sports person using Chinese. Your partner and yourself will work on writing questions and answers in Chinese. Rehearse the Interview and be ready to present the Interview to your teacher.

Useful sentences:

你叫什么名字？

你几岁？

你是哪国人？

你喜欢什么运动？

你会打………吗？

More useful questions for your Interview:

- When did you first start playing...?
- How often do you play...?
- Why do you like playing....?
- Where do you play.....?

Get started: Write your first draft here and get feedback from your teacher and classmates before you rehearse the Interview.

_____
_____
_____
_____
_____
_____
_____
_____

Tea

According to legend, tea was first discovered by the Chinese emperor and inventor Shennong, in 2737 BCE. It is said that the emperor liked his drinking water boiled before he drank it so it would be clean, so that is what his servants did.

One day, on a trip to a distant region, he and his army stopped to rest. A servant began boiling water for him to drink, and a dead leaf from the wild tea bush fell into the water.

It turned a brownish color, but it was unnoticed and presented to the emperor anyway. The emperor drank it and found it very refreshing, and cha (tea) was born.

Learning Activities

1. Have a tea-tasting session with your students. Encourage students to describe drinking the different types of tea.

2. Students create a Newspaper Review of each tea tasted.

3. Bring to the classroom, a variety of tea-pots and cups. Allow students to examine the artifacts and make a drawing of each one. Students can also label the teapot and cups using Chinese.

Language Content

| 茶 | 茶壶 | 茶杯 |
| chá | chá hú | chá bēi |

我喜欢喝茶 | 我不喜欢喝茶

Terracotta Warriors

In the Ch'in Dynasty about 210 BC, one of the emperors had a whole army of men made out of clay to go in his tomb and guard him in the afterlife.

To make a head like the ones the emperor buried in his tomb, build it out of clay. It will use less clay if you make an armature - a core made out of something else. You might use a balloon, or crumple paper into balls and then cover them with tape.

For more than two thousand years, Chinese children have heard fantastic stories about China's first great ruler, Emperor Qin Shihuangdi. The stories told about a great army made up of terra-cotta soldiers and of a burial tomb filled with jewels and magical rivers that flowed to the sea.

In 1974, the Chinese made an amazing discovery—the stories about Emperor Qin and his great army, are not fantastic at all; they're true. An army of more than eight thousand soldiers made of terra cotta, a baked reddish clay, is buried fifteen to twenty feet beneath the earth not far from the tomb pyramid where Emperor Qin is believed to be buried along with riches of his dynasty.

People learned by accident that the stories about Emperor Qin were true. Farmers digging a well in a field struck the head of a terra-cotta soldier. News of the discovery quickly spread, and archeologists swarmed to the site in the central Chinese province of Xian — 西安. After much effort was spent drilling core samples from the earth, archeologists learned that about eight thousand terra-cotta warriors were buried in chambers beneath the ground.

So far, archeologists have dug up and pieced together about one thousand of the soldiers. The soldiers were damaged by raiding rebel armies shortly after their creation and also by the collapse of heavy roof timbers over time. Also uncovered were about one hundred wooden war chariots, about six hundred life-size terra-cotta horses, and thousands of weapons. The soldiers stand about six feet tall, and each appears to have its' own individual personality.

Learning Activities

1. Using clay or playdoh, create your own Terracotta Warriors.

2. Research the Terracotta Warriors and find interesting images to share with the class.

Language Content 兵马 俑 *bīngmǎ yǒng*

Tian An Men Square

Finding Tian An Men Square

Give directions in Chinese from:

1. 天安门 to 北海公园

2. 天安门 to 北京动物园

3. 天安门 to 美术馆

Transport in China

Learning Activities:

1. Research what bus and train tickets in China look like. Students will use the information to create their own Chinese tickets.

中国高速铁路

2. Find out all you can about the High Speed Rail system in China. Using a map of China, outline where the high-speed rail goes. Plan a three-day itinerary for a tourist to use the high-speed railway system.

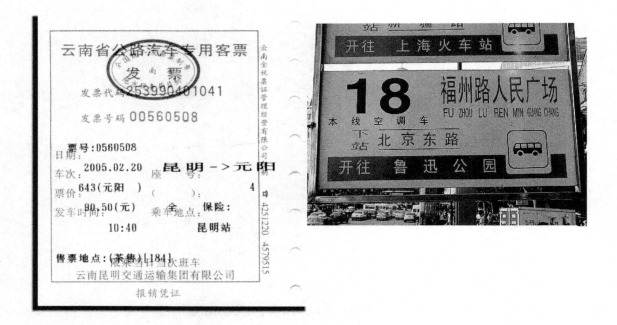

3. Conduct a survey in Chinese of your classmates to find out how they get to school. Compare your results with how Chinese students travel to school.

4. Make a list of words you will need to travel on a bus in China. Use the words to create your own role-play with a classmate. Perform the role-play to the whole class.

Umbrellas

Chinese umbrellas are the earliest known umbrellas used, and have existed for over 2,000 years. In the beginning, Chinese umbrellas were made of silk, and later paper umbrellas were created.

The Chinese lacquered and waxed their Chinese umbrellas to repel water, so they could be used in the rain. They were among the first to do this. The frames of most umbrellas in China were and are made from bamboo or mulberry bark. The Chinese painted their Chinese umbrellas as well.

The royal families typically carried red or yellow umbrellas while the common people would carry blue ones.

Design a royal umbrella below:

Can you say this rhyme?

大头
大头，
下雨不愁，

人家有伞，

你有大头！

Zodiac

The **Chinese Zodiac** is determined by the **Chinese Lunar Calendar** and is based on the cycles of the moon, unlike our western or Gregorian calendar, which is based on the solar cycle.

The **origins of the Chinese Zodiac** go back a few thousand years. According to the myths, long time ago, **Buddha** decided to call all the animals on earth. But only twelve came:
- the Rat
- the Ox
- the Tiger
- the Rabbit
- the Dragon
- the Snake
- the Horse
- the Goat
- the Monkey
- the Rooster
- the Dog
- the Pig

Buddha assigned each of these animals a year on the cycle affirming that children born in that year would acquire the personality traits of the animal assigned to that year.

In order to decide their **order in the Chinese Zodiac cycle,** the animals held **a very exciting race.** The first one to cross the river would be granted the first year, the second to come in would be the second animal in the cycle, and so on.

Learning Activities

1. Read the Chinese Zodiac legend to students and introduce the animal names in Chinese. Assign a Chinese character to each student and ask them to draw the animal. Create a large mural of each animal and label in Chinese.

2. Ask all students to make each Chinese character into the animal it represents.

Language Content

你属什么?

Nǐ shǔ shénme?

87

Chinese Zodiac

Rehearse these questions and answers with a friend.

你属什么?
我属。。。。。。

你是哪年生的?
我是。。。。年生的。

你几岁?
我。。。岁

The Story of the Chinese Zodiac

Many people have wondered over the years how it was that the rat, the smallest of all the creatures, was given the honour of having the first year of the Chinese Zodiac named after him. This is the story I have heard.

A very long time ago, the Jade Emperor, who ruled the heavens of China, sent a message to all the animals asking them to come together so that he could give each of them a year, which would make it easier for the people of China to keep track of time. The cat and the rat were good friends and decided to travel to meet the Jade Emperor together.

When it came time to leave, however, the cat was taking a nap. The rat, realising that he would have to use all his cunning to be noticed by the Jade Emperor, left his friend sleeping, and set off on his own. This is why there is no year named after the cat, and also why cats have hated rats ever since.

When the rat arrived, the Jade Emperor welcomed him and the other animals and told them that they should all take part in a swimming race. Once again, the rat realised that he would have to be very clever if he wanted to win the race. He found the largest, strongest animal, which was the ox, and pleaded with him to let him ride on its head. The ox was kind and strong, and agreed that they would swim across together. The rat travelled safely across the river on the ox's back, but, just before they reached the other side, climbed over the ox's head, jumped onto land, and reached the finish line first. The rat had proved its cunning, and the Jade Emperor named the first year after the rat and the second year after the ox.

Zòng zi Recipe

粽子

1. 50 sheets of bamboo or reed leaves
2. Glutinous rice (1 kilogram)
3. Chinese dates (250 grams)

Directions

1. Soak the rice and the dates 12 hours or more till they are soaked thoroughly.
2. Wash the leaves.
3. A chopping board is necessary for laying out the leaves.
4. Fold the leaves flat at the leafstalk to make a sheet.
5. Hold the sheet, fold it round in the middle and make a funnel till both ends are laid over each other in one direction.
6. Use about 1/10 kg. of rice and 6 dates for each dumpling. The dates must be covered by the rice so that they won't lose too much syrup in cooking.
7. Fold the leaves up to seal the open side of the funnel and tie the bundle with a band made of twisted leaves. Make sure that the bundle is tied neither too tight nor too loose. This helps make sure that the ingredients are well cooked.
8. Put the dumplings in a pot, cover with water and make sure they are pressed and kept still while being boiled.
9. Cooking time: 40 minutes in a pressure cooker; 2 hours in an ordinary pot.

Rehearse these sentences and questions with a Talk Partner.

我喜欢吃粽子。

我不喜欢吃粽子。

你喜欢吃粽子吗？

我最喜欢吃粽子。

Zong zi - Can you write the Chinese character?

粽	子		
粽	子		
粽	子		
粽	子		
粽	子		

Printed in Great Britain
by Amazon